Are You a FISH?

by THOMAS KINGSLEY TROUPE

amicus LEARNING

illustrated by MARTINA ROTONDO

Steve was a sunfish. Just five minutes ago, he heard someone say an odd word.

"Watch out for fish," Dexter the dragonfly buzzed to his friend.

"What's a fish?" Steve asked.

"Forget it," Dexter said. "We're out of here!" He and his friend flew away.

He couldn't forget it.
Steve truly wanted to know.

"Vertebrates are animals that have a backbone," Spike said.
"Alas, I do not."

Steve made a note about vertebrates.

Steve came across Talulah the turtle.

ARE YOU A FISH?

Talulah laughed. "I'm no fish, mister," she said. "Look at my eyes. I've got three eyelids. One of them is clear!"

"Nice," Steve said.
"How many do fish have?"

"None!" Talulah cried. "Fish with eyes don't need them! The water moistens their eyes."

Steve added no eyelids to his notes.

Steve found Preston the pig at the farm.

"Are you a fish?" Steve asked.
   Preston snorted. "Gosh, no," he said. "I'm warm-blooded. Almost all fish are cold-blooded. They can't keep their body temperature the same like I can."
"Is that bad?" Steve asked.
"Yes, if the water is too hot or too cold," Preston replied.

Steve wrote down cold-blooded in his notebook.

Steve swam over to Roxy the raccoon.

"ARE YOU A FISH?"

Roxy shook her head. "Oh please," she said. "I'm not a fish. I have beautiful fur all over my body."

"Fish don't have fur?" Steve asked.

Roxy shook her head. "Sorry, little guy. Fish have slimy, smooth skin. It's kind of gross."

Steve jotted slimy, smooth skin in his notepad.

"How do gills work?" Steve asked.

"Water *passses* through *gillsss*," Sissy said. "And the *gillsss* grab the oxygen *fisssh* need to breathe!"

Steve made a note about gills.

Steve saw Georgia the gnat flying around.

"Are you a fish?" Steve asked.
"Are you kidding me?" Georgia cried.
"No! I don't have a swim bladder!"
"What's a swim bladder?" Steve asked.
"It's like a balloon inside a fish's body," Georgia explained. "The air inside the bladder helps keep fish stable underwater."

Steve added swim bladder to his notes.

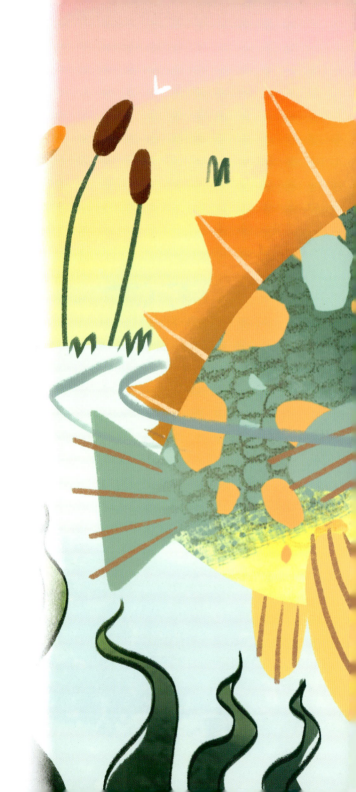

"No," Hannah said. "But I do like a bird bath!"

Steve wrote notes about water habitats.

Steve dove deep into the lake. He saw Fernando.
"Hold up," Steve gurgled.

"That's right, genius," Fernando said. "I've got fins just like all fish do. They help me swim fast."

"Yes!" Steve shouted. "I found a fish!"

Steve followed Fernando deeper.
There, he saw other fish with backbones. They had gills and fins.
They were underwater. They had slimy skin.

"Are you all fish?"

"You bet," Belinda the bass said, smiling.

"Wait," Steve said. "That means I am, too!"

20

Steve's Notebook

FISH . . .

- Are vertebrates. They have backbones.
- Don't have eyelids.
- Are cold-blooded.
- Have slimy, smooth skin.
- Have gills to help them breathe underwater.
- Have swim bladders to help them float in water.
- Are aquatic. That means they live in water!
- Have fins to help them move in water.

GLOSSARY

aquatic Living or growing in water.

cold-blooded Having a body temperature that changes to match the surrounding temperature.

fin A part on the body of a fish shaped like a flap that helps a fish move through water.

gill Either of a pair of organs near a fish's mouth; fish breathe through gills by taking in oxygen from the water.

warm-blooded Having a body temperature that stays about the same no matter what the surrounding temperature is.

WEBSITES

BioKids — Kids' Inquiry of Diverse Species — Ray-finned fishes

http://www.biokids.umich.edu/critters/Actinopterygii/

Fish: National Geographic Kids

https://kids.nationalgeographic.com/animals/fish

Fish | San Diego Zoo Animals and Plants

https://kids.nationalgeographic.com/animals/fish

Every effort has been made to ensure that these websites are appropriate for children. However, because of the nature of the Internet, it is impossible to guarantee that these sites will remain active indefinitely or that their contents will not be altered.

READ MORE

Owen, Ruth. *Animal Classification.* Minneapolis: Bearport Publishing Company, 2024.

Schell, Lily. *Fantastic Fish.* Minneapolis: Bellwether Media, 2023.

Simons, Lisa M. Bolt. *How Are Animals Grouped?* North Mankato, Minnesota: Pebble, 2022.

AMICUS ILLUSTRATED is published by
Amicus Learning, an imprint of Amicus
P.O. Box 227, Mankato, MN 56002
www.amicuspublishing.us

Copyright © 2025 Amicus. International copyright reserved in all countries. No part of this book may be reproduced in any form without written permission from the publisher.

Library of Congress Cataloging-in-Publication Data
Names: Troupe, Thomas Kingsley, author. | Rotondo, Martina, illustrator.
Title: Are you a fish? / by Thomas Kingsley Troupe ; illustrated by Martina Rotondo.
Description: Mankato, MN : Amicus Illustrated, [2025] | Series: Animal classification | Includes bibliographical references. | Audience: Ages 6–9 | Audience: Grades 2–3 | Summary: "When nosy Steve the sunfish overhears Dexter the dragonfly saying to watch out for fish, Steve sets out on a mission to find out what exactly a fish is. After interviewing other animals and learning about the characteristics of fish, Steve realizes that he too is a fish! Includes fact page, glossary, and resources for further research"— Provided by publisher.
Identifiers: LCCN 2024010602 (print) | LCCN 2024010603 (ebook) | ISBN 9798892001151 (library binding) | ISBN 9798892001731 (paperback) | ISBN 9798892002318 (ebook)
Subjects: LCSH: Fishes—Juvenile literature. | Fishes—Classification—Juvenile literature. | Animals—Classification—Juvenile literature.
Classification: LCC QL617.2 .T76 2025 (print) | LCC QL617.2 (ebook) | DDC 597—dc23/eng/20240405
LC record available at https://lccn.loc.gov/2024010602
LC ebook record available at https://lccn.loc.gov/2024010603

Printed in China.

Editor: Rebecca Glaser
Designer: Kim Pfeffer

ABOUT THE AUTHOR

Thomas Kingsley Troupe is the author of more than 200 books for young readers. When he's not writing, he enjoys reading, playing video games, and investigating haunted places with the Twin Cities Paranormal Society. Otherwise, he's probably taking a nap or something. Thomas lives in Woodbury, Minnesota, with his two sons.

ABOUT THE ILLUSTRATOR

Artist since always, Martina Rotondo attended the Master of Illustration and Concept Art at The Sign Academy in Florence, Italy. She currently works as an illustrator for both Italian and foreign publishing houses. Lover of traditional drawing, she is also constantly researching and experimenting with new techniques to create her surreal and engaging characters and backgrounds.